VAMPIRES

Matthew Haigh is the author of *Death Magazine* (Salt, 2019) and *Black Jam* (Broken Sleep Books, 2019). He is the co-editor of *Hit Points: an anthology of video game poetry* (Broken Sleep Books, 2021). *Death Magazine* was longlisted for the Polari first book prize in 2020. His work has been highly commended in the Forward prizes, commended in the Winchester Poetry Prize, and published in journals including *Poetry Wales*, *The Rialto*, *Magma*, *Fourteen Poems*, *The Guardian* and *Poetry London*. Further work has featured in anthologies from The Emma Press, Bad Betty Press and Sidekick Books. He has performed at a number of festivals including Cheltenham and Gloucester Poetry Festivals, Swansea Fringe and the European Poetry Festival. In 2021 he was a judge for the Poetry Wales Pamphlet Competition and interviewed for *Edge Magazine* on the relationship between poetry and video games. Matthew lives in Cardiff.

Vampires

Published by Bad Betty Press in 2021
www.badbettypress.com

Cover design by Matthew Haigh

Printed and bound in the United Kingdom

A CIP record of this book is available from the British Library.

ISBN: 978-1-913268-21-3

Supported using public funding by
ARTS COUNCIL ENGLAND
LOTTERY FUNDED

vampires

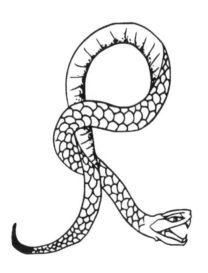

BAD BETTY PRESS

Vampires

For Rachel

Contents

The NewZealand Story

The memory is this: a vast crystal whale, a pixel-plump bird in the belly. My brother and I lovebirds in your crystal room. Your CDs sprouted a forest of fingerprint spirits from all the child-soft touches. Always adventurers, brothers – always dashing to the ends of worlds. Acid fractals reconfigure the whale to weeping gut. Your weight is whale song.

I Am Your Witch

Playing dress up and you a giant mouth
rosy globes of bone.
In this bedroom universe my head's blonde moon
orbits the planet of you.
Such forests of makeup we pushed through
to find the witch within – you set obsidian lakes
on my nails, chalked twilight across my cheeks.
You never forget
the bin bag's crinkle as it's taped around your body
in lieu of a costume, the waxy green effulgence
of fake fingers. Full chest.
You spun me around toward October burning
the night so buttered with amethyst.
This boy, you took his mind
you let the gender-bending bats in
let the spider eyes in.
Sweeps of eyeliner –
slashes between seductive worlds.
I play your cassette tape that raises a light-cage over us
that wards off memory loss, which is the true death.
I was born raw as whale fat –
horror movies licked their blood light over me.
Once you stood in the kitchen
lopping a glistening *pineapple* down
to gold-hoop earrings.
We could smear the word pineapple
with your ashes and it would mean something.

Once, god was stuck to the stuccoed ceiling of that house
like a white-gloved hand. A mouse pointer.
Playing Nintendo, we shriek with laughter
as we kick bombs back and forth
you shouting *I'm dead* so many times as if rehearsing
for the big day, as if tempting fate – the way
a moth invites itself to your lips.
The one thing I keep is the vial of nail polish.
I'm thumbing the black crust off it
when the call comes through
when mum's howl stabs
upwards from the hallway
but I'm getting ahead of myself –
I meant only to talk about the time I went as a ghost
into the dripping night
your warmth followed me.
Tarmac exhaled from fresh rain
dark as liver
your fingers at my back
I swear for a moment my trainers
left the mirrored ground.

I said *I want to go as Catwoman for Halloween*

They told me I was a boy. Pick the Penguin instead. If only we possessed better vocabularies as children. I would have said "I will inhabit this planet for a smudge a rind a wafer-skin of time and you're telling me I can't be a BDSM vixen with an opal face and legs for days?"

Sundays

You undress Barbie's soap-sliver body, slide neon leggings from rubber. I imagine the interior of my skull scented like a doll's head, factory perfume, candyfloss. Do you know how much I want to pinch that toy stiletto between my teeth – to swallow my girlishness?

Beauty pours off the face of the truly content and as you fashion doll clothes I feel your warmth pooling, a permed silhouette, the careful work of ceremony played out with bobby pins, thread, off-cuts of leopard print –

and I was there, for a time – in the steam from a Sunday roast, in the seat of your love, in the rolling combs of light.

VHS

my birth was bonfire smoke and roads slicked back like Black Jacks
/ two hearts bat-curled to cinema's dark / we watched *The Lost Boys*
/ felt the electric horses of plasma through our blood / I'm thinking
beaches / buckles on leather / soaked in rain's god-breath as we dance
around / fire swatch spitting sparks from a steel drum / nothing can
touch you now and your flesh's pearl cake / elation is a drunk thing
/ we can never die / childhood is leaping from a bridge into mist /
Rachel / don't dream without me

A Tarantula Is Like a Heart, They Both Explode When Dropped

You died first in Thornton's, toffee-knived. Sweet brittle
slit your throat; peanut gold spilling out. From death you were reborn pink and raw like a tarantula kicking off its ghost.

We guessed that the resurrection had been painful – when we mentioned it, you'd hiss *SHUT UP!* Love, how useless we were – how little impact our words had.

Hardboiled dreams rolled to you, summoned children, essential buttons. You died next all creamy, fingers coral-tipped from crumble.

Doctors milled about milk-bottle smooth, alien. Mouthing *cholesterol.* You swore this was the turning point. Rebirth's ectoplasm swam on your skin.

You died last, in this reality, with a hundred secret ways to eat, veins thick with cherry Slush Puppie.

Idol

We could not prevent you being golden. Grudgingly, granddad babysat while you went to Weight Watchers. We watched *Jaws 3D* without the 3D; the fish was a sideways paper nightmare. Someone said they saw you alone in Burger King. Afterwards we toiled, scrubbing you down to remove the caked-on gold, speaking the healing words by rote. The Midas light always fluttered back to your cheek.

Nostalgia

gothic Venus in your clamshell armchair / sometimes we could not take you with us / with ear cocked to kitchen door I'd hear the adults talking / there was no room in the car / your weight would break the suspension / so many discussions around the space you occupied as if a planet had come to tea or a problematic statue required respite / the projectionist's light chucks handfuls of diamonds over us / there's a fat ghost in the movie *Casper* and the word the characters snarl is *fat* / the word we'd so often hear lobbed about, ricocheting off the walls white-hot / coming to rest at your feet where it would lay / inert and useless

Whoopi Goldberg

Like a precious gem dissolving, she trades the glitz and glamour of lounge singer life for the convent's pale slate. Brother, we sit in the car listening to the soundtrack on cassette. Swaddled in a parka while silence powders the back seat, I drift from myself. I nose at the prospect of conversation from the heart the way a deer picks through snow. Your tongue is a trigger – my insides bolt. *Sister Act* plays across a dozen TV channels and brother we are deathless. When viewed again and again a movie warps the concept of time – how can we have aged when Whoopi's skin is always smooth as gold lake water.

At the Core of the World

think silt water / think cherubic face of porcelain doll / think broken pieces peeking through / half a red smile / that's what recollection is / at family gatherings we were webbed with light / smeared and sherbet dabbed with it / softness from all sides / maternal in the yolk / this light my brother is what you now claw back to when you make lists of retro video games / in *Zool* the ninja claws down through the earth / layer upon layer / and beneath the membrane of soil / at the core of the world / is such brilliant candy

16-bit Music

chartreuse windchimes of Mega Drive / shifting to synthetic griddle /
hellish red drills / I once ripped your spinal cord from your torso and
it was love

Versions of Heaven

The beta version:

was Ritz Video. I picked a cartoon that turned out to be anime.
The first time I heard the word slut was from the mouth of an
elf.

Version 0.9:

was brothers pelting toward Blockbuster, luminous with tie-dye,
taking it for granted that you'd be close behind.

Version 0.9.1:

was a simulated paradise, the air heavy with Parma Violets (I
tried not to picture your violet skin vanishing into a body bag).

Version 1.0:

was your heart ripe as sunlight, still issuing orders of love, still
sweeping its fleets of blood-bikes down arterial highways.

Version 1.0.1:

was the hazel hood of your eyes, on loop.

Version 1.0.2:

saw me creep across your room, slide open drawer upon drawer
aglisten with chocolate tombstones.

Version 1.1:

I leaned in for a kiss – the baby powder cloud you wore like a
visor, breaking its canopy as if inhaling a new planet.

Version 1.1.1:

> was a Boglin for a fist. All 90s toys were toxic and smelled fucking great.

Version 2.0:

> was a factory, chocolate bars clad in cloaks of chrome. Milk Pond. Dream Cream. Camel Butter. You probed the foil door open with your tongue, followed the galaxy down.

Version 2.0.1:

> was the butterflies alive in your hair on route to Barry Island. Black sacks of Kodaks. You, plunging through the log flume's spume in your velvet coffin.

Version 2.0.2:

> was the exercise bike; untouched. Dancing to *True Blue* in your room.

Version 2.1:

> was the unveiling of your new body – a soap bubble, chromatic disc. An eye in space.

Version 2.1.1:

> was you middle-aged, glorious, heart as tough as pig skin. Spilling ebullient from your skirts, girls.

Hologram

Memory, you are an absent father. When you open a suitcase to remove sheaths of glass lit with holograms, shuffle and spread them before me, I cannot trust you. I was not always so sweet. She once shrank in the doorway from my poison tongue. What demonic enzyme was it swam inside her that we could not reach – could not burn or burst with loving words. I believed that just by fizzing around wild and aglow like all children I might convince her to live for me. In the garden, after dark, she piled on more hot dogs – each one a thick meat bullet sizzling with her name.

Parma Violets

you're inside the wedding cake
coffin of icing / violet frosted roses
do you want me to hug you in heaven forever?

> I plunge a hand inside the mess
> of sponge to pull you out
> did you see that episode of *Buffy*

where they resurrect her dead mum
but she's not quite the same?
your soft hand is like that / you don't speak

> I had a dream filled
> with beautiful spooky music
> the sky was end-of-summer blue

I walked streets paved with vinyl
and *Smash Hits* magazine looking for you
when I woke there were no cake crumbs

> and that music never existed

Mr Whippy

the vampire of time shot one bloodshot eye through a mirror / saw you
/ sped a fang aflame through your vein's highway / 44 was scrawled
through one suicidal incisor / all through life the cream cake your
companion / all through life the red sauce / time puts its mouth to us
and feasts and we feast from earth's dream / fuck it / let me be invaded
by the same death snow / the same dreadful emperor / let me be
buried in a coffin filled with sugar / we'll go the same way / cramming
crushed pearls down our throats / the past is a party in a glass room
sunk through the ocean's never / your gothic locket is lowered /
lowered and gone / this space is where you reign / coquettish face
split to cochineal parts / glass flutes curdling shake / accordion flesh
arrayed across dimensions / you queen of mirrors

Desert Peach

(i)

Belinda Carlisle in the cold sun / beach sunset sets fire to plum sorbet hearts

(ii)

      low tide lures a thousand tears to the gut
the moon an orange bloom / the magnet singing to the soul's sodium
                this is Americana's sun-bleached system / experience
via the brain
                        leafing through its movie archive

(iii)

a kingdom is drawn around a carpet / belly down / eyes flicked up to
the TV's moon

      certificate 18 meant *nowt* as nan would say
                so chromatic horror flickered in the tides
                            of my face

(iv)

dusk holds hot magic / sodium through the lounge / cats turn on carpet
                                          beached whale babies

your movie paused at twenty / you stopped going out
                                    you lived via easy Earth girls

        plastic pearls
                        Americana's sun-bleached kingdom come to
dust

(v)

in the Pantone book of colour death rubs shoulders with plum sorbet

death is not glass or glacial / glass is at least something
                                              the shades fade from
            mint eye shadow to banana split sundae
                                          your shade is
        the funfair's pureed light

(vi)

       I hold in my mind the poles of you – the poster with Elvira's
plum lipstick
the My Little Pony / relic of god

                                how were you here then not / how
      was the pony's arse infused with butterscotch

(vii)

leafing through the brain's archive / colour is the first to go
        the shade that blooms
                in the mind's tide is desert peach / how it swarmed you
in summer

      sodium sorbet turning cats to sand bodies

(viii)

your house of glass a liquid oozing with the flow of light / a thousand
        sun-bleached carpet weaves / a thousand golden worms
                                         tiger stripes in the
haze

(ix)

this is what the gut sings / a kingdom of rust / a bracelet of kids
                                       riding their bikes into sky

(x)

taped to the cover of a magazine / an edible worm in a lolly / bronze
curl suspended
        in a glass heart / I worked my tongue around it / licking and
only eroding
those edges of nothing
            how the nothing shrank / dissolved
                                    bringing the worm into focus
        how the years after a death shrink

                              bringing you into prominence

Two Hands through Time and Space

i saw it go up from your body........

........a purple light...............................

auntie........a flare........a flickering diamond........

...............................with your smile inside...............

i saw it leave you........auntie........a bad shock...............

...............here........let's wipe your eyes........put the kettle on

...............................we'll steel our sobs with sweetness...........

...................i want to go back...........

........to the moment that sparked your spiral........

the first time someone called you fat......................................

...............first time you felt the crack........of chair leg...................

.......................cross the bridge of your nose...............

...........i want...........to be there........when it comes down from space that sour meat seedpod............ravenous god............

..................................auntie............I would kick it...............

....across the car park

........find you as a child crouched beneath the table cloth

........i would take your hand................lead you away.............

.... o drug of stolen sugar.............

...............................let's draw up the covers............

........................auntie............switch off your torch

Acknowledgements

Many thanks to the editors of the following publications in
which past incarnations of these poems have appeared: *Poetry
Wales*, *Impossible Archetype* and *Fourteen Poems*. 'Desert Peach' was
commended in the Winchester Poetry Prize 2020 with the title 'The
Colour of Death is Desert Peach.'

Thank you to Amy and Jake at Bad Betty for believing in the work,
and to Chrissy Williams and Stephen Sexton for their generous
endorsements. Thank you to John McCullough for providing
feedback on an early reading of the manuscript.

The biggest love to Omar, Alex and Mum for always supporting me.

Lightning Source UK Ltd.
Milton Keynes UK
UKHW010748061021
391723UK00001B/58